Praise for

Take Back the Smile that Cancer Stole

"You might think a book called, Take Back the Smile that Cancer Stole, *would be a difficult or perhaps depressing read. However, I found the book to be both enlightening and inspirational. As a friend of Dr. Ron, as well as a cancer survivor and fellow author, I agreed to read Ron's book and give him my honest opinion. What I pleasantly found was a book that not only provides a straight forward explanation as to the ravaging effects that cancer and chemotherapy can have on a survivor's smile, but it also shares some real-world examples of what can be done to restore one's smile, and therefore their confidence.*

"Dr. Ron chose to focus on an area of dentistry that is not only hard to pronounce, it's also hard to understand – until this book! If you, or someone you know, has had their smile impacted from cancer, please make sure they read this book, and more importantly, make sure they reach out to meet Dr. Ron, a man who has dedicated his life to helping his patients restore 'the smile that cancer stole.' You'll be glad you did."

~ Jim Palmer,

The Dream Business Coach

www.GetJimPalmer.com

"A cancer diagnosis consumes your life; the immediate response is to get into treatment right away and get rid of the disease. It's hard to imagine that life's joys still exist, but they most certainly do. Cancer wreaks havoc on your body and this includes your mouth and teeth. Dr. Koslowski, or Dr. K. as patients call him, explains how your mouth and teeth are impacted by cancer and provides expert advice on how to include dental hygiene in your treatment plan so that you can live your life to the fullest. Smiling helps you feel better and it's important to maintain your smile through your treatment, so it can shine bright afterwards. This book is a must read for people diagnosed with cancer, caregivers and medical professionals."

~ Ann Marie Potter, PhD,
Registered Occupational Therapist,
Cancer Survivor, Cancer Advocate

To my parents, Bea & Eddie, who taught me to care for and respect others.

To my children, Chloe & Madison, who keep me young and fill my life with laughter.

Table of Contents

Foreword

For more than 20 years, I have been taking care of cancer patients with radiation therapy and chemotherapy. Cancers of the head and neck region remain one of the most challenging diseases. Both emotionally and physically, I have been amazed by the strength and bravery of our patients who go through this difficult journey. Most of the times, our patients win their war on cancer. However, there is a price to pay to become a survivor. There are side effects especially in the oral cavity region. These side effects can be very challenging and need a dedicated team.

This specialized team focuses on the care of each unique patient whose personalized treatment starts with communication between all the oncologists (surgeon, medical and radiation); the dental oncologist; and other necessary team-members. We strive for eradication of cancer with optimal quality of life. But, it takes a "village" to get there!

The dental oncologist and his staff take care of our patients in a unique way. Their care starts before the treatment starts, continues during the treatment, and of course it continues for years after treatment is completed. I have worked with Dr. Ron Koslowski for 10 years taking care of our patients. I communicate with him before the treatments start regarding the goals, dosage and fields of radiation. We also discuss types of chemotherapy or if targeted therapy is planned and other factors which can affect the treatments. This communication is coordinated through our weekly tumor board conferences where we review all the radiology and pathology information. Each patient is discussed in a multidisciplinary format among all the oncologists team and the plan of care is coordinated. Sometimes, there may be a special need for teeth extraction. These are done in an expedited manner by the oral surgeon to allow time for healing before treatments start.

This communication continues during the treatment course. It includes coordinating the mouth shields/devices or fluoride trays which may be needed for radiation treatment setups. Proper oral hygiene cannot be over-emphasized. It is extremely important, especially since patients may have mouth sores, dry mouth and poor taste. Some of these effects are temporary and will resolve in a few weeks.

After completion of chemotherapy and radiation therapy, we follow our patients very closely. One of the most important reasons to follow-up is attention to dental care. Xerostomia (dry mouth) is one of the main side effects which can improve over the years. During this time, patients are at high risk of dental caries which is decay and proper follow-up and oral hygiene remains extremely important. The communication with a dental oncologist continues during this journey to recovery with the best quality of life.

Dr. Ron Koslowski does an excellent job of explaining all this in *Take back the Smile that Cancer Stole.* I have been honored to be working with him to help our patients in their journey of becoming cancer survivors. We have seen many patients winning back their smile, and our team looks forward to seeing many more winning smiles.

Afshin Safa, MD

Assistant Professor,

Department of Radiation Oncology

David Geffen School of Medicine at UCLA

Medical Director,

Harold Pump Department of Radiation Oncology

Northridge Hospital Medical Center

Preface

Nice to Meet You!

Your life was going along just fine, taking in all that Southern California has to offer with trips to the beach, games at Dodger Stadium and those warm, nighttime summer concerts. But something happened. Your world was rocked the moment you found out that you had oral cancer.

Uncertainty struck and suddenly you began sifting through medical terms that were new to you while trying to understand the treatments. Yet, you mustered your courage, fought off cancer and now you're called a "survivor." You'd love to share your joy except cancer took something precious away from you—your smile.

Get Your Smile Back. That's Why I'm Here.

I chose a little-known specialty in the wider field of dentistry called *prosthodontics* to help oral cancer patients like you regain the ability to smile, to step out in public confidently, and to feel at ease when having those all-important and highly relational one-on-one conversations with people who are important to you.

Your condition is one that I'm well-acquainted with and how it affects you is important to me. My practice is based on the desire to help others become their very best since I know that your oral health affects so many areas of your life.

Guess where my interest in dentistry and caring for people started? Travel back with me and see what led us to cross paths at this moment in your life.

It was another world, but one that grabbed my attention and wouldn't let me go. The starship Enterprise hurtling through space carrying its fearless crew. Like many kids my age, I tuned in *Star Trek* to experience the next adventure with the crew. One man in particular became my hero, Dr. McCoy. When someone was sick, he healed them and his dry sense of humor made him likable.

Critics have called Bones "the heart of the Enterprise crew." He was the one who wanted to do the right thing. Kirk had the mission, Spock his logic, but what McCoy cared about was his patients. That struck an important chord with me.

Boys in my Los Angeles neighborhood and at school wanted to grow up to become firemen, baseball players, the President, and actors, but helping people ranked high on my list. And I found that desire fulfilled in the one place that scares folks—the dentist's office, a place of wonder. When I got my teeth checked and slid into the dentist's chair, the bright lights and equipment like drills didn't frighten me. Instead, I was fascinated by the dentist poking in the mouth and using a cool little mirror to look in the out-of-the-way places for cavities. Patients got their sore teeth fixed and walked away with mouths that were fresh. Amazing.

Compare that with a neighborhood liquor store. My parents owned a market and liquor store in Beverly Hills and they made a lasting impact on me by treating others with respect. It was a true "mom and pop" store and my very own mom and pop set high standards by caring for each of their customers. Some of the people who came in were recognizable celebrities that were used to being *oohed* and *aahed* over.

Guess what? The many customers who weren't in films or TV got the same treatment. My parents gave everyone star treatment. I spent hours in the store as a child, working on my studies and I worked there as a teenager seeing firsthand how they took care of customers. Eventually, I wanted to combine my family's entrepreneurial spirit with my respect for the dental profession. Even though the businesses were extremely different, the attitude of valuing people was the same.

After college, I went off to dental school where I embraced the profession and wanted to soak up all the knowledge and experience around me.

You Are Why I Do What I Do

I'm a *dental oncologist* who is here to help and I've made my office a safe place. I'm here to care for your mouth before, during, and after your treatments for oral cancer. My desire is to be your ally at this time that is so important for your well-being. You've heard lots of terms from a variety of professionals. You've been surrounded by technology that was unfamiliar to you. But at the heart of it all, the health profession is one of people reaching out to help others on their journey to be whole.

When we talk about good health and wellness, we're treated to images of people eating fresh vegetables and running in the park to boost the heart rate. But the mouth and the role it plays in our well-being doesn't get much attention.

This book is for your benefit to show you how good oral health is worth pursuing. You'll notice some *Big Word* alerts along the way to convey information that's accurate and useful. Our mouths are amazing treasures, but little information is shared about them in popular culture. We're told to brush our teeth regularly and see the dentist every six months. There are more exciting things to learn. Your mouth is the gateway to your health and I want to show it off to you. Come along!

Chapter One:

Your Mouth: Home of Your Smile

Now let's talk about something that makes you unique and shapes how others see you. Can you guess what that can be? Here's the answer: your teeth.

Your teeth are similar to the beams and other supports that give shape and attractive lines to a beautifully crafted home, and your gums are the foundation that gives your teeth stability. A specialist like myself who knows your diagnosis and the impact on your mouth's structure is able to help your smile reach its full potential.

You should understand how your teeth and gums work together to help you. So come along on a tour and I'll guide you each step of the way.

Do you ever think about what you're seeing and learning when you go on a tour?

Universal Studios is fun with the corny spiel from the tram driver. How about the Getty Museum off the 405 freeway, Mammoth Caves in Kentucky, or historic Williamsburg, Virginia? In each of these completely different settings there is design and structure that leads to beauty and wonder. Let's get a close-up view.

"Big Word Alert: Prosthodontist"

It's only fair that I share a bit more about my qualifications so you can be assured that I'll take you on the right path. Of course, getting lost in your own mouth would be something to write home about.

Yes, I've gone to dental school and gotten good grades like so many caring men and women. I also went a step beyond that to get a hard-to-pronounce specialty, *prosthodontist*. It really means that I'm an architect of the mouth. Just like a contractor who knows the plumbing, electrical and roofing systems to build a house or repair it, I've learned the systems that make up this part of you that no one else can copy.

That's right. Lots of people have mouths but your smile is unique among all the billions of people sharing our planet. Your teeth and gums have a *function* and create an *appearance* that reveals a lot of who you are. Your teeth aren't just for chewing food. I want you to have a better understanding of your mouth so that you can feel comfortable with the work that I do before, during, and after treatments. Dental care ultimately helps create the healthiest you possible.

> ***"We shall never know all the good that a simple smile can do:"***
>
> ***~ Mother Teresa***

As we get started, think about this.

Why is the Universal Studios tour popular? *You're getting a behind-the-scenes look* of the special effects and sets that create the movies that we watch. We appreciate how the films are made and it enhances our movie-going experience. A tour in a cave gives us a different look at the earth, and a restored colonial town of Williamsburg gives us an appreciation for how men and women worked and lived—and we can see how their ingenuity led to the lives we enjoy today.

Appreciating your mouth is appreciating your health.

Let's discover how your gums, teeth, saliva and bones offer clues as to what's happening throughout your body. Think about this. If you see someone dressed well, you may think that what you notice first is their clothes or how fit they appear. Something else is happening. If they have a beaming smile, their eyes light up and their attractiveness skyrockets. That's why the mouth is such a fascinating area to get to know. So come along and who better to have as your tour guide than a prosthodontist?

Inside Your Smile

How you smile reveals a lot of who you are – the person inside, which is what we refer to as your personality. A healthy smile can wear away over the years because your mouth is a battleground, a place of invisible drama with forces fighting to wear down your enamel and healthy tissues. You become tempted to shrink back and not smile as much, but you can come out on top with extra care.

Your mouth isn't just a *grind 'em up* and *swallow 'em down* factory that munches food and gulps beverages.

It's the gateway to your body's health, the first step on the journey deep into the digestive system. We've heard the fun song about the anatomy, "The ankle bone's connected to the shin bone. The shin bone's connected to the…." You get the idea. I can't stress enough how our oral health truly does impact the rest of our body.

> **"Sometimes your joy is the source of your smile, but sometimes your smile can be the source of your joy."**
>
> **~Thich Nhat Hanh, Zen Master**

Chewing your food well allows whatever is inside your meal to get absorbed into your organs and bloodstream. If you eat vegetables and lean proteins, then your body will absorb the vitamins and minerals that come from whatever you have prepared. If your mouth can't function well then the nutrients won't absorb and give you as much benefit.

The connection in our bodies is similar to the plumbing in our homes that let water flow from the sink or bathtub and drain away in a well-designed system.

Teeth

Our first stop is the teeth and they have lots of work to do every day. Teeth and dentists go together, don't they, like peanut butter and jelly? You get a cavity and the dentist fills it, puts a crown on it, or may perform a root canal. But we're going to look more deeply, and during this tour we'll begin to see why specialists like myself are necessary.

Teeth give structure to your facial appearance like steel girders in a high rise, and they have two main parts called the crown and root. When you speak, your teeth play a key role in how clear you sound.

Hard enamel coats the outside. The Dental Foundation of Ireland notes that the enamel is hardest surface in the body, but it can decay. Eat a piece of candy and drink a soda. The sugar is potent and eventually wears down the protective covering if it's allowed to sit on the teeth undisturbed.

It may look like your teeth are just sitting in your mouth, but did you realize they're vibrant and alive?

Below the enamel is the dentine, a mineralized layer of living tissue and beyond that is the root canal, or *pulp chamber* which is home for blood vessels, cells, and connective tissue. It's like a pipeline to transport nutrients from the bloodstream to the dental fluid. You can see how our bodies aren't just separate parts, but instead are a related whole. This connection from the bloodstream to the teeth is why we can look in the mouth during a dental exam to see the health of your body.

Of course, your teeth will never just get up and walk away because they're secured to the jaw bone by thousands of tiny ligaments. Talk about miniaturized technology; our mouths were far ahead of our smartphones and watches.

Gums

"Big Word Alert – Oral microbiome"

Now let's look at the gums, another part of your mouth easily seen when you laugh or talk up close and personal.

Just like plants take root in soil, your teeth take root in the gums. These do more than act as a holder for your teeth, they're a natural barrier against the hundreds of microorganisms trying to enter the body through the mouth. Your gums are made of a soft tissue that covers the bones around your teeth and forms a tight seal that then supports the bones.

Gums offer a picture of one's overall health.

You know those weather maps on TV that show high pressure and low pressure systems with weather conditions across the country? The gums are a bit like that map. In your mouth is what we call an *oral microbiome*, a complex ecosystem of bacteria. When all the species are in balance then the gums are protected from disease-causing bacteria. But throw off the system and pathogens invade. Inflamed gums will bleed and can lead to further periodontal disease. Advanced gum disease has been linked to conditions ranging from heart issues to irritable bowel syndrome.

Your gums are durable and they're put to the test every day. Not only do they ward off bacteria, but they can be damaged by the very act of brushing teeth. How? When you're in a hurry, have you ever just taken your tooth brush and ran it quickly through your mouth? The bristles can hurt the gums.

In grade-school, you got lessons in flossing and brushing your teeth. Adults need to get reminders, too, since improper techniques can tear the gums. We'll cover more on keeping your teeth and gums clean and healthy in Chapter Six.

Bacteria

"Big Word Alert: Streptococcus mutans"

"Big Word Alert: Porphyromonas gingivalis"

So what happens to that food? Think back to the last time you ate chicken. You take a bite, chew it, swallow and you can feel a little that's stuck between your teeth. Little particles snuggle into the crevices between the incisors or back along the molars. How about a potato chip? It's smaller but tiny fragments get caught.

No big deal, right? My advice is you need to act like there's a sign with red letters that says, "No loitering. This means you food particle."

If the particles aren't removed, then they camp in one spot and turn into bad bacteria. Think about this. Ever go camping? Clean showers and restrooms are a prized item at campgrounds since they make us feel refreshed. You know what the opposite is like. It becomes a bad scene and campers give poor reviews.

Don't let your mouth be like a nasty campground. Refresh it often by getting rid of the bad bacteria. That's why we brush our teeth and floss regularly. Eat plenty of veggies that give nutrition and enjoy drinking water. This is a "natural" approach to the problem.

Think of sodas, fruit juices, candy and fatty foods coated with grease. If that's what you eat and drink then your mouth becomes like an old, clunky RV that's filled with brackish gunk. You're bringing in unusual elements, outside forces, that can breed bad bacteria. You won't find concession stands on this tour offering French fries or deep-fried Snickers like they have at the county fair, so if you get thirsty drink some water or munch on an apple.

Let's travel into the world of bacteria, hidden from plain sight.

You pull back the tab on a can of Dr. Pepper or Coke and sip it or gulp it down. It slips so easily down the throat and tastes great on a hot day. You finish the can and say, "all gone." Not quite.

Residue from the drink settles on the teeth, and then do you know what happens? Bacteria like *Streptococcus mutans* feeds on the sugary coating. This type of bacteria is among the "bad" ones that are fed by sugar and starchy carbs. It's the main cause of tooth decay and other oral diseases because the acid produced erodes tooth enamel.

It's not just your teeth that get affected. Your gums are targets, too. When they get diseased look out for this strain with a long name: *Porphyromonas gingivalis*. You've heard of *gingivitis*? It's inflammation of the gums and left untreated it can lead to gum disease that destroys gum tissue and the alveolar bone that supports your teeth.

A single mouth can house more than six billion bacteria, living from about seven hundred strains, and many are helpful microbes, probiotics, that can support your oral wellness and overall health.

The pathway to decay takes time, as you know. If you drink a soda today and forget to brush your teeth before going to bed, it's not like you'll have obvious tooth decay tomorrow. It will happen, though, if you don't develop good habits. Patients with special conditions like yours are at a greater risk than their friends and family. Please don't wait. If you've been diagnosed for oral cancer then know that decay can happen in your mouth more quickly than in the general population. Caring for your mouth becomes mission-critical to maintain your smile, the health of your teeth, and the overall health of your body.

The toothbrush doesn't remove six months of tartar 30 minutes before your appointment.

Yes, you're busy. You barely have enough time in the morning to put your hair in order while quickly running the toothbrush across your teeth. Who has time to floss when you're running kids to school or making a mad dash to the office?

So what happens? The bacteria have a nice undisturbed place to begin its work and eventually you notice you have a cavity or your gums are tender.

Brushing properly and flossing regularly are truly important tasks. And talk about cost-effective. A toothbrush and floss that only cost several dollars are actually tools that improve your health.

One more thing. Drink water and stay hydrated. Here's why.

Saliva

Just like caves have underground rivers running through them, our mouths have their own pool of fluid known as saliva. For over 2,000 years, doctors in various societies have used it to diagnose health issues. It is a "complex fluid," as noted in an article "Science Behind Human Saliva" in the *Journal of Natural Science, Biology and Medicine*. It "influences oral health through specific and nonspecific physical and chemical properties." That's a mouthful to think about.

Here's one more truth that shows how our bodies are closely connected as one unit and not just separate parts. Your teeth grind up what you eat and your saliva has mucus that binds the food you chew so it slips easily through the esophagus. Keeping your mouth moist is simple to do and it's so important.

In Chapter Four, I'll share more on why you should avoid dry mouth. I don't want you to just think, "Oh, yeah. I'll drink some water now and then." I want you to notice if your mouth feels dry and I want you to be aware so that you're drinking plenty of water throughout every day. Staying hydrated is as important as brushing and flossing.

Saliva does something else that's important. Have you ever driven along a dirty, dusty backroad? You know how your car or SUV looks at the end of the trip. All filthy and grimy. So you take it to the car wash and clean off all those little dirt particles that can eat away at the paint. Guess what? You've got a car wash inside your mouth with your saliva. The liquid helps wash away inflammatory bacteria and keeps the little crevices a bit cleaner.

Have you ever been to a beach where there are tide pools? Waves come in and wash over the water, then recede and life blossoms in the little pools of water. Saliva is a life-giving fluid that all of us need. So celebrate with a nice glass of water.

What happens when your mouth isn't moist? You wake up with "morning breath" because your mouth dried out as you slept. Bacteria camped out and had its fun.

Yep, Spit Happens—Here's Why

Lots of information and clues about your mouth are found in your saliva. Analyzing it gives us clues about health at the cellular level. It's not just spit we're talking about. We can detect cancer and know the causes of other conditions like acne and even male pattern baldness. Where does all this fluid come from?

You have glands in and around the oral cavity that secrete liquid just like water bubbles up out of the earth through springs. Saliva contains so much information about your health that you could compare it to the internet.

If we could read the stories of diagnostic information present within saliva, then the abundance of information waiting to be found could be comparable to a vast vault of information such as the internet. The relationship between salivation and behaviors within our daily lives is undeniable. Yet most people never appreciate the uniqueness of saliva.

Your Jaws of Life

"Big Word Alert: Mandible"

"Big Word Alert: Maxillofacial Prosthetics"

Imagine we're walking down a set of stairs on our tour to the jaw. You might think of this bone as more a part of the face and not the mouth. It has a working partnership with what happens inside the mouth. The lower jaw, known as the mandible, forms the lower part of the skull and the upper jaw, the maxilla, completes the mouth structure. Now you can understand the name of my sub-specialty, *Maxillofacial Prosthetics*.

Next time you're at a Dodgers game, and that walk-off homer wins the game for the Boys in Blue, look at the people sitting nearby. Their jaws are allowing them to shout and cheer. Next time you're at dinner, notice how your jaw works in helping your teeth chew food. Your lower teeth are rooted in the lower jaw and if they decay your jaw bone can eventually feel the pain. This bone doesn't move on its own. Four muscles move it up and down and side to side. These are the:

- Masseter: connects the jaw to the cheek bone and its job is closure
- Temporalis: this closes the jaw, elevates and lowers the mandible, helps move the jaw side to side
- Medial Pterygoid: protrudes the mandible and aids in grinding movements
- Lateral Pterygoid: works with the medial pterygoid for side movements and grinding

I could go on and on about the fascinating way your mouth with all its parts is connected to your well-being, but you can, uh, *digest* what you've just read for now.

Mouth tours do happen with me in real life. When a new patient comes to my office, I carefully take note of what I see to determine their overall health. I'll check the teeth and gums and then make sure their mouths are staying moist. The jaws, palate, tongue—I scan it all, using my knowledge and real-world experience to check their health.

I know every patient is different in how much information they want to hear and process. I'm willing to go in to as much detail as needed to help you understand what's happening so you become aware that caring for your mouth will make you a healthier person.

Information can empower us and I'm here for you. And, yes, many dentists are familiar with the workings of all these systems and how bacteria affect your insides. For those who are going through oral cancer treatments or have had them, something more potent than Hot Cheetos has entered your oral microbiome. We're not just talking food particles stuck between your teeth. Let's see what happens during your chemotherapy and radiation treatments.

Recap:

- There's much more to your mouth than your smile, but your smile is unique!
- Your teeth give structure to your face, like steel beams; however, unlike those beams, your teeth are alive and vibrant.
- Gums do more than hold your teeth; they are a natural barrier against thousands of unwanted microorganisms.
- Get rid of unwanted, nasty bacteria with consistent good dental health practices.
- Saliva is like a car wash in your mouth – consistently cleaning.
- Your jaw has a working partnership with what happens in your mouth.

Chapter Two:

Oral Cancer Overview

You are a wonder, built one cell at a time. Your body, as you know, is made up of cells and these are the building blocks that make up tissues. Your mouth's environment is sensitive yet well-equipped to fight off unwanted bacteria. But there are forces that enter and disturb the balance. In Chapter One, we toured the most visible parts of the mouth but now we're going to peek way down to the cellular level. As we do, this will help you understand cancer's impact and why you benefit from an experienced professional handling your oral care.

Starting Small – How Cancer Starts

"Big Word Alert: Squamous Cell Carcinoma"

"Big Word Alert: Opharyngeal"

When all is going well, normal cells grow and divide to form new cells as the body needs them. When normal cells grow old or get damaged they die and new cells take their place. New cells that the body doesn't need, and old or damaged cells that don't die as they should, become extra cells that form tumors –a mass of tissue.

Cells in your mouth are known as *squamous cells.* They are flat and cover the surface of the mouth, tongue and lips. Cancers that begin here are called squamous cell carcinomas.

If you took a helicopter ride over any part of Los Angeles, the sprawling freeway system would stretch for miles with cars constantly on the move—going from the congestion of surface streets and onto freeways. You'd also see clumps of cars at mall parking lots and office complexes. Watch for a bit and then you'd see the vehicles pull away on to the streets and the freeways. We're constantly on the move, dynamic.

Oral cancer cells don't sit still, either. They can spread by breaking away from the original tumor. They enter blood vessels or lymph vessels which branch into all tissues of the body. The cancer cells often appear first in nearby lymph nodes in the neck.

The floor of the mouth and tongue is the location for about two-thirds of cancer of the mouth, but it can hit in the upper or lower jaw, lips, gums, and cheek lining. Another form of cancer, *oropharyngeal*, occurs in the back of the tongue, tonsils, and throat tissue.

How did this happen?

Your mouth's environment was thrown out of balance. For most oral cancer patients there are three main causes: tobacco use, alcohol, and HPV16, the human papilloma virus, or any combination of these elements. HPV is the same virus that causes cervical cancer. My hope is that with the use of HPV vaccines that all children should be receiving, there will be a protective effect from oral/pharyngeal cancers caused by the virus.

For now, let's look at the cancer treatment. Caring for your mouth becomes more important than ever.

Working to Stop Cancer

Left unchecked, cancer will have its way. It'd be like the New England Patriots playing a game without an opposing team on the field. The scoreboard wouldn't be able to tally all the points. Okay, for those of you who don't like the Pats you can insert any sport and any team playing a game without an opponent. *The team that's unopposed is going to win.* And that's how it is with cancer.

Let's introduce chemotherapy and radiation. Imagine them running through the stadium tunnel and onto the field to stop cancerous cells from spreading. Why do we use them?

> **"You can be a victim of cancer, or a survivor of cancer. It's a mindset."**
>
> **~ Dave Pelzer**

Chemo is a mixture of anti-cancer drugs working through the whole body. Radiation uses high-energy waves or particles to combat the cells. The goal, as the American Cancer Society has said, is to slow the growth of the cancer for as long as possible and to help relieve any symptoms the cancer is causing.

You don't need to go too deep into the science behind chemotherapy and radiation, but it's good to have a starting point for understanding how the treatment works. You know what happens during a football game played on natural grass? The field gets torn up and the grass has to be replaced. The tussle that happens during treatment also alters your mouth's environment. Always remember, *staying committed to good oral health is your pathway to being whole.*

How Chemo Works

Cell division is important in detecting cancer. Professionals spend their careers studying cancer cells so addressing it here will be basic and simple. Healthy or normal cells stop dividing when coming into contact with cells that are like them. That's not the case with cancer cells. They keep dividing. They die when they're unable to divide.

There are two types of chemotherapy. One type targets cells that are dividing and the other targets at it when the cell is at rest. Cells also have a self-death called *apoptosis*.

Chemotherapy is given in cycles and is based on variables including the type of cells, the rate that the cells are dividing and the time when a given drug is likely to be effective. Chemotherapy is most effective at killing cells that are rapidly dividing.

Now, here's a challenge. Chemotherapy doesn't know the difference between cancer cells and the normal cells. The delicate balance in your mouth gets thrown off until the normal cells grow back.

Radiation tackles cancerous cells in a more targeted way.

About half of newly diagnosed cancer patients will receive radiation combined with either surgery or chemotherapy. Radiation gets inside the cancer cell and damages the DNA. All cancer cells with DNA damaged beyond the cell's ability to repair will eventually die or stop dividing. But just like chemotherapy isn't smart enough to know the difference between types of cells, radiation can affect healthy cells near the targeted area. The lining of the mucous membrane inside the mouth, oral mucosa, is especially vulnerable.

Working with patients who have oral cancer is my specialty and it's beneficial for them since I understand how both the cancer and treatment impacts their mouth's environment.

Those wonderful salivary glands that produce such an effective cleansing fluid aren't going to be as powerful. Some foods won't taste as great and you're opening the door to possible infections.

Some dentists who are seeing patients undergoing cancer treatments may see something in the mouth and say, "Hmm, let's keep an eye on that" while I could look at the same condition and say, "Let's take action."

I've been fortunate to have a career that gives me the foundational training as a dentist, plus a specialty in knowing the structure of the jaws, teeth, and gums. My work as an architect of the mouth is enhanced by my working knowledge of cancer to help patients maximize their health and restore important functions.

The Obnoxious Neighbors

Having cancer and undergoing treatment to get rid of it is like living in a house with an obnoxious neighbor on one side and a vigilant neighbor on the other. One side is the disease and the other is the cure. You decide to get to know them and you invite them over for a cookout, hoping they'll appreciate your manicured lawn, new patio, and fresh-looking furniture. You soon discover that when the obnoxious neighbor eats, he tosses his trash around on the patio, tramples in your flower beds, and just doesn't give a hoot about your place.

The vigilant neighbor loses his cool and gets into a tussle with the bad guy, muscling him out, knocking into a fruit tree and kicking over a trash can in the chase. After they leave, you're left with a mess and it's time to clean up and fix any damage done. You set out to clean things up, replant your flower beds and restore your lawn. And you make a note to never invite the obnoxious one over again.

> **"Cancer didn't bring me to my knees, it brought me to my feet."**
>
> **~ Michael Douglas**

That's a simple illustration of the tussle between the cancerous cells and the treatment. Once it's all finished, you'll have some restoration work to do and I'm here to help.

Peaks and Valleys

In Southern California, we're fortunate to have a number of scenic mountain trails. Drive up Highway 2 in the winter, the Angeles Crest Highway, and you can often see a series of snow-capped peaks to the east. It's a beautiful sight. You and I both know that when you're hiking toward a peak, you're going to walk in a zig-zag pattern up steep grades, dipping low, and zigzagging along switchbacks. It's easy to lose sight of your destination and wonder if you'll ever get there.

Setting off on treatment for oral cancer is like a new journey. Sometimes you'll feel a dip in energy when undergoing chemo and radiation treatments for head and neck cancer. It's like you're heading into a valley and here's why.

A couple of weeks into a cycle of chemo, the white blood cell count drops to a low level. Infections flaring up as fevers are common, including what are referred to as "fevers of unknown origin." This doesn't surprise me or any of the health professionals who are involved in your care.

Your immune system is becoming suppressed and that's a common occurrence. We understand what's happening and we're going to work closely with you to keep you focused on your goal of reaching optimal health and putting your place back in order. And, as an oral cancer patient, that place is your mouth.

Recap

- Oral cancer – squamous cell carcinoma – typically results from your mouth's environment being thrown out of balance.
- Chemo and radiation therapy are the typical treatment options and disrupt cancer cells' ability to continue dividing.
- Cancer cells die when they can no longer divide.
- Loss of energy, due to a drop in your white blood cell count, is a common side effect.

Chapter Three:

Dental Oncology

Preparation is key. You've learned that since childhood. If it was raining outside, then you'd take an umbrella to stay dry. Teachers helped you prepare to take tests and coaches helped you get ready to compete.

When you're prepared, you can face your days with confidence. If you've not yet started your chemo or radiation treatments, then I'm able to help you prepare by receiving a thorough dental exam. Here are three important reasons why an exam benefits you:

- You'll reduce your chances of systemic infection
- Improve your overall oral health
- Decrease your long-term cost of care

And while a general dentist can examine your teeth, *I'm equipped as a dental oncologist to understand what's happening with your mouth due to your diagnosis.*

Knowing what's happening with your condition can help you take smart steps. We take precautions all the time. Using sunscreen when outdoors protects your skin, while an alarm system that notifies authorities in the event of a home break-in is another level of security.

So much happens in life that we can't stop or prevent so a key principle to adhere to is taking control whenever possible. If the weather forecast predicts heavy rain, you carry an umbrella, or at the very least wear a jacket or coat.

Your mouth is an asset that's worth protecting like your car, home, and other valuables.

A prosthodontist like me, provides safekeeping for your mouth. Those of us who have a specialty in working with cancer patients can see possible complications before therapy starts. Together, you and I can address those issues and then your treatments won't have to be interrupted.

Why Visit a Dental Oncologist

You have a choice to make as you get an exam before your treatments and for your care after you finish. Should you use a general dentist you know and trust or visit a dental oncologist? It's true that dentists are schooled on the basics of oral cancer during their education and they're taught what to look for. Many of my patients, though, are referred to me by their general dentist or other health professionals where treating oral cancer is outside the scope of their expertise.

The foundational look at cancer that all dentists receive is helpful when examining patients who are diligent in getting their teeth cleaned regularly, like every six months. Consider this: if the very beginnings of a cavity are developing, then many dentists will want to "watch and wait" to see if the condition worsens. Oral cancer patients need a different approach.

You are in a different category. Remember what you read in Chapters One and Two. Someone who has a head or neck cancer, that obnoxious neighbor, has a disruption to their mouth and its environment. The use of chemo or radiation alters the mouth in a way that's different than someone who has never had that diagnosis.

When conditions are changing, just like wind is whipping flames in one direction and then in another, a wait and see approach doesn't help you. Oral cancer can affect one patient differently than another.

> **"If you fell down yesterday, stand up today."**
>
> **~ H.G. Wells**

Few dentists know the detailed workings of the cancer cells, the impact of treatments, and how to go about maximizing a patient's health. That's why I'm able to examine a mouth before treatment and accurately assess the condition. I'll identify problems and prioritize them. Some things may need immediate attention while others can wait. I'm equipped to help in accurate and high-quality restorations once treatments are finished.

I'm a dental specialist, a prosthodontist, with extensive training in the sub-specialty of Maxillofacial Prosthetics. All of this has given me the privilege of knowing in great detail how the teeth, gum, saliva, and jaw are affected and how to help patients.

Before Treatment Begins

Schedule an exam about a month before you begin chemotherapy or radiation. That way, if we have to do any procedures, the area worked on will have a chance to heal. Any conditions that already exist such as abscesses or gum disease can be made worse during treatment. Again, I want to work with you to prevent infections and ensure that no complications will flare up that could interrupt your therapy.

About 40 percent of all cancer patients, not just those with oral cancer, will have some sort of oral complication. So working with a professional like myself is more than a good idea. It's strategic. My work enhances your quality of life.

The mouth is such a small area of our body, but you are different from any other dental patient. You're in a vulnerable state. Since our bodies are a connected whole, an infection in your mouth can have an effect throughout your body. Having a dental exam from a professional thoroughly schooled in dental oncology helps to address any possible sources of infection before starting cancer treatment.

What to Expect in an Exam

If you've been diagnosed with oral cancer, then I'm going to check and make sure all oral structures are in good condition. We want to know the current situation so that problems don't arise during treatments.

During a full prosthodontic examination, I'll look in the hard and soft tissues for what *should not* be there:

- White or red patches
- Sores, irritations or lumps
- Numbness of the tongue or other areas of the mouth
- Swelling of the jaw
- Difficulty chewing, swallowing or moving the tongue or jaw

X-rays of your mouth will reveal the condition of your teeth. I'll look for any fractured teeth, identify concerns like periodontal disease and address sites of potential infection. Teeth that can't be restored should be extracted at least two weeks before your treatment starts. Orthodontic bands and brackets, if any, will be taken out.

A professional cleaning done before treatment will remove bacteria, plaque and tartar. This further reduces your risk for infection. Some of your teeth may have cavities. These should be treated if the exam is made with plenty of time before your treatment begins. A small cavity, however, can likely wait if time doesn't permit and you have a lot of specialty appointments. I can take care of those after treatment is finished and make it part of your care plan.

> **"Perseverance is not a long race; it is many short races one after the other."**
>
> **~ Walter Elliot**

You'll also come away with a thorough

understanding of how to care for your mouth by maintaining adequate nutrition and practicing the best oral hygiene possible.

It's a complete work-up in this important step to regain your health. Quality oral care plays a role in successful cancer treatment.

Communication

Another reason to choose a dental oncologist is that it makes communication easier with other specialists who are treating you. Caring for an oral cancer patient brings together health professionals who have different disciplines. We each have a working knowledge of cancer. I speak the same language and have their same orientation. If you have questions, then I can explain your concerns to the other professionals.

Here's a way to think about it. You get on a plane and fly from Los Angeles to Denver. It takes an array of men and women who are committed to their jobs to make the flight happen. And if it's a pleasant experience, then so much the better. Pilots, air traffic controllers, flight attendants, mechanics, baggage handlers, and agents at the gate along with maintenance workers (and the people who make those little bags of pretzels) are involved in making sure you get off the tarmac in LA and land safely in the Mile High City.

Working with Other Specialists

"Big Word Alert: Obturator Prosthesis"

A multidisciplinary team is often helpful. Head and neck cancers are different than those that affect other areas of the body. Your facial appearance is possibly impacted but your speech may be, too. My training as a cancer specialist allows me to communicate with and understand the work of many specialists:

- Oral Surgeons – removes teeth that can't be restored
- Periodontists – gum care specialists
- Endodontists – root canal specialists
- Pathologists – this specialist will make a microscopic examination of the affected area to determine if the affected cells are cancerous

If the cells are cancerous, then planning begins for the best possible treatment and outcome. This is when a complete dental exam by me is useful since doctors usually advise patients to have dental work done before treatment begins. If possible, schedule about one month before starting treatment. That way, if any invasive dental procedures are necessary your mouth will have a chance to heal.

- Radiation Oncologists – may ask me to make a shield if the patient's tongue or jaw has to be in a certain position
- Speech therapists
- Reconstructive Surgeons
- Head and neck surgeons who are working with the upper jaw and the palate, will ask me to assist them in the operating room. An appliance I can make and place immediately is a surgical

obturator prosthesis that provides closure in the mouth and helps the patient in speaking and eating. You can read about it more in Chapter Four.

What You'll See in My Office

Your oral health is my priority and your care will be customized to your condition and given with personal attention as you'll notice when you visit my office in Encino. I'm not in a medical complex but in an easy-to-access building. I have a private room to discuss your condition as necessary and a few exam rooms, similar to what you'd see in your dentist's office. I also have a small lab where I can specially design solutions. You'll get the attention you need and answers to the questions on your mind.

And, yes, I have sugar-free candies near the front door. Go ahead and take a couple. They taste good and they'll help keep your mouth moist.

Now that you've had your initial exam, you're ready to proceed with treatment. As you go through chemo and radiation, remember that I'll be waiting so we can create a post-treatment plan that works well.

Common Occurrences

So you're aware, here are common issues that occur in the mouth when having chemo, radiation, or a combination.

- Mucositis / Stomatitis: the mucous membranes become inflamed.
- Infections that are viral, bacterial or fungal can occur.
- Dry mouth, or salivary gland dysfunction. This simply means that your saliva production is reduced.
- Chewing and swallowing can be challenging as well since the muscles won't be as elastic and food might not have all the taste and flavors that you've become accustomed to.

Doing simple things like sucking on ice chips and chewing sugarless candies or gum will help provide the all-important moisture. Now you can begin treatment with confidence. Once completed, we'll move on to the next steps related to your care so you'll want to grace the world with your smile once again.

Recap

- Preparation is key. Prosthodontists work with cancer patients to uncover possible complications before therapy starts.
- Because all cancers and every patient is different, prosthodontists have much greater experience with the disease than general dentists.
- Ideally, schedule an exam about one month prior to the start of chemotherapy or radiation treatment.

- Pre-treatment professional cleaning helps reduce the risk of infection.
- Your prosthodontist can serve as a gateway to and liaison with other needed specialists.

Chapter Four:

Maintaining Oral Health

Treatment is designed to stop the spread of cancer, and now we're going to do everything we can to keep your mouth healthy and vibrant. But before we get into the specifics of how I've treated patients, I hope you can tell that I appreciate who you are and the condition that you're going to battle. A patient of mine, John R., summed up my care for others from his perspective, "as an older guy with cancer, there's a tendency for doctors to 'blow you off' but Dr. K has treated me with the utmost respect and that, coupled with his craftsmanship, is pretty fantastic."

You're in a vulnerable state, but my office is a safe place where you'll be welcomed. Now let's get started with your care now that you've gone through cancer treatments. I'll lay out guidelines that are proven beneficial. I was interviewed for a video by the American College of Prosthodontists and I gave them my perspective that caring for your teeth and mouth is quite special. This isn't just about catching a cavity here or there. My quality of care handles significant issues, like reducing and preventing breakage of the teeth and protecting restorations.

Consistency

Coming in for a regular cleaning is your first step. You've heard it said that most people should see the dentist twice a year, every six months. For oral cancer patients, we step that up a bit. Like every three months and it has wonderful benefits. Take a cue from one of my patients, Gabe.

Gabe had tonsil cancer and he successfully went through his treatments. He came to me for follow-up visits, and my hygienist and I showed him the importance of good dental hygiene. But he slacked off. Not surprising. We all have full schedules and a visit to a dentist can easily be pushed aside if you have other events and activities needing your attention. We didn't see him for a while and then it happened. He had to have a couple of crowns replaced because of his tooth decay.

Personal experience is a master teacher.

Gabe decided he was going to take control, just like a homeowner clearing brush off his property. He wanted to prevent further decay and started visiting the office every three months. He's a pleasant man who likes our friendly team and it's been a pleasure to work with him.

Your condition is different than most everyone else you'll meet, but you're certainly not alone. Regular cleanings can sound so basic that you may wonder if they'll be effective. I've seen patients stay as healthy as possible with consistent and frequent visits for thorough cleanings and exams. The reason is we're removing the bad bacteria before it can do its damage. Remember, our bodies are a whole unit and your mouth is a connected environment with all the parts working together.

Dry Mouth

"Big Word Alert: Xerostomia"

A common condition that oral cancer patients share is dry mouth, known as xerostomia. If you only did one thing after chemo and radiation to prevent infections and decay then *keeping your mouth moist is absolutely the smartest thing you can do*. Remember this before treatment, during treatment and after treatment: water is your friend. Drink it with enthusiasm.

Dry mouth happens because your treatment impacts your salivary glands and you end up producing less of that wonderful saliva that so many take for granted. Moisture really does impact an environment. Think of the northeast where the hills get plenty of rain. Trees are green, the ground is soft, and planting a garden is easy to do. Now, think of a place like Palm Springs, Needles or Blythe where they only get a few inches of rain a year. The ground has a completely different quality and growing a backyard garden requires a plan to irrigate and add nutrients to the soil.

When your mouth is dry, a more acidic environment than normal develops and affects the mucous chambers.

Saliva has a buffering and cleansing quality. When production is reduced, food is more likely to stick in between and on the surface of the teeth. Bacteria can grow more easily since there is less saliva to wash it away and then heavy plaque develops. Staying hydrated with water helps and now is the time to use special products like Biotene that are formulated for your condition.

What happens if saliva production is reduced and your mouth is dry for too long? Tooth decay sets in quickly. Remember, you are in a different category of care than other dental patients and it's important that we catch any decay early. Prevention is such a key to maintaining your overall well-being. Regular brushing and flossing is a task that you can do every day, but a skilled dental hygienist is a tremendous support for you. A skilled hygienist knows how to floss and clean properly and gently for your condition.

Stopping the decay as early as possible helps you maintain healthy teeth. Now let's give special attention to patients who have had radiation treatments.

Where Your Teeth Are Planted

Your teeth are rooted in the jaw bone. When you've received certain amounts of radiation, then pulling decayed teeth may not be an option because the jaw bone may not heal properly. The patient I mentioned earlier this chapter, John R., is a health professional. He came to me after having radiation treatments. Serious tooth decay had already set in and a few of his front teeth had already broken off. A "flipper" had been placed inside his mouth by his previous dental professional and then he was referred to me. I made a new flipper for him and he's much happier with it than with his previous appliance.

Here's another benefit of a prosthodontist compared to a regular dentist.

I worked carefully with the radiation oncologist to see where it was safe to pull teeth from John's jaw bone and where we had to leave them alone.

I have the training and scope of experience to assess and work with these unique conditions. Plus, I was able to make him a customized appliance to replace his teeth and he's very happy with it. John also understands that regular oral hygiene care empowers him against tooth decay and infections that can surface. Dry mouth is a challenge for him as well, but because he's faithful in his care, we're able to catch cavities here and there and help him maintain the best health possible.

> **"Self-empowerment is seeking the solution rather than fixating on the problem."**
>
> **~ Coach Bobbi**

Successful post-treatment care is a concerted effort between my patients and me.

What about the rest of John's teeth? I certainly won't take a "wait and see" approach. We actively monitor the situation and maintain the roots in the bone. For a tooth that needs help, you can't always pull it, but a patient can go for root canal treatment. That becomes safer than pulling in areas that have had a lot of radiation.

You can understand how some of the decisions that I make as a dental oncologist are vastly different than those made by a general dentist.

The mouth is a sensitive place to work and not everyone who sees me has had chemo or radiation. Mary comes to mind. She had a benign tumor on her palate so she didn't need radiation, but she had surgery. The procedure left her with an opening in her palate and that made speaking and eating very difficult. Food and drinks simply didn't digest properly and sometimes came out through her nose. But I was able to help her. The solution was making a customized denture called an obturator for her with an extension to close the opening.

Restoring the missing function for Mary was deeply rewarding. When she speaks, family and friends can understand what she's saying and now she can eat and drink in public without feeling self-conscious.

So much of what we've handled has happened inside the mouth, but think back to our tour at the beginning. Your jaw bone is a significant feature that provides structure. Radiation can weaken it and if tooth decay sets in then the area becomes fragile. It's great to know what can be done to restore the lower jaw so implants can be used. A fibula free flap, or free tissue transfer procedure, is used to reconstruct the mandible when part of it has to be removed for cancer surgery. Surgeons use bone from the leg, say the fibula in the calf, along with the skin and muscle, and graft it in. It's new bone that hasn't been radiated, so implants can then be used and a patient's quality of life is enhanced with the reconstruction.

Implants can be put in at the time of the surgery with a head and neck surgeon and a plastic surgeon working at the same time. After the restoration and healing, I can make a bridge on the implants.

Patients have thanked me for my craftsmanship and it's a high standard that I embrace. My profession allows me to combine artistic work with scientific knowledge—all wrapped up with a love for people. Sometimes patients come to me to correct work that was done by other dental professionals. Either the procedure didn't go correctly, or the restorative device simply didn't function in the contours of the patient's mouth.

A man in his sixties who came to see me originally had radiation treatments for lymphoma when he was 17 years old. Back then, the radiation field throughout the mouth was more wide-spread, and not as targeted as today's 3D technology that allows us to pinpoint treatment and avoid healthy teeth as much as possible. When he came to me, he was developing another cancer and had trouble opening his mouth. He could only open 16 millimeters. To put that in perspective, 40 millimeters is typical.

He had state-of-the-art reconstruction on his lower jaw, yet there were complications with his soft palate. The appliance that was made for him broke and his speech therapist recommended that he see me. To speak properly, the soft palate has to be able to move and close the airway, so I fashioned a new appliance to be able to do just that.

You can see how oral cancer requires professionals of different disciplines working together and how I'm able to communicate with a variety of people who care for a patient's health.

Here's a look at some of the restorative tools and treatment aids that I can make.

Some patients will need specialized dentures and I can craft those. Prosthetics that I make restore these life-giving abilities to overcome cancer and the resulting treatments. That's my motivation. I'm thrilled every time I see patients regain their confidence while knowing I've played a key role in their health and social enjoyment.

Restorative Tools

FLUORIDE TRAY

Purpose: Delivering prescription-strength fluoride gel directly to the teeth

Here's something I highly recommend as part of one's oral hygiene and to combat dry mouth. It's a custom fluoride tray that I make in my on-site lab. Simple but more effective than using a brush-on paste. Use a prescription fluoride on the tray then put it on the teeth for five minutes and don't rinse for a half hour. Do it every day and you get the same result as a professional fluoride treatment in the office. Fluoride treatments strengthen tooth enamel and battle against the acids from plaque that cause the loss of minerals.

This simple tool is effective in tackling the issue of dry mouth, not as severe a side effect it once was thanks to advances in radiation treatment. Some of the salivary glands are spared and that's great news for the patients. However, someone can also think their condition isn't too severe, and since they don't feel uncomfortable they may not take the proper steps to stay hydrated. The problem is that plaque builds up on the teeth and the acidity increases in the mouth. So you may feel fine, but this imperceptible battle is taking place inside.

This is a basic step, but so important. Regular check-ups in my office that are more frequent than typical dental patients, drinking plenty of water, and the daily use of a fluoride tray will work wonders in helping combat the bacteria that causes tooth decay and gum disease.

SHIELD

Purpose: Protecting tissues during radiation treatment

A shield during treatment is useful to minimize effects. I can make one and will work with the radiation oncologist to know what part of the mouth or throat will receive the radiation. The tongue may need moved out of the way or protected. Sometimes the jaw has to be in a certain position to get the maximum benefit of the special radiation field and protect other parts of the mouth that don't need radiation.

In Chapter Three, I mentioned that there are times when I'll go into the operating room to assist the head and neck surgeon. The purpose is to always get the best result possible for the patient. I did this for a patient, Sonia, who had work done on her upper jaw, affecting her palate.

After the surgical dressing is removed I'll make an obturator that helps in eating and speaking. The shape of the palate is going to change over the coming months so a temporary version is made. This allows the patient to speak without sounding hypernasal, and allows for eating more easily than if the custom obturator wasn't in place.

Here are different types of obturators that can be used, depending on the need.

Surgical Obturator Prosthesis: covers palate and is used after surgery to provide closure.

Interim and Definitive Obturator: covers palate and restores the teeth and gums. It has an extension which aids in swallowing, eating, chewing, and speaking.

Palatal Lift Prosthesis: helps soft palate assume correct position for speech.

Palatal Augmentation (Drop) Prosthesis: alters palate prosthetically for speech.

Mandibular Resection Prosthesis: replaces portion of the jaw that has been lost and restores gums and teeth.

Each customized, personalized approach ensures the patient gets the best outcome possible.

Developing a forward-looking view is helpful. I'm looking at the present as I scan your mouth with an understanding of the future. The healthier your mouth and teeth stay now, then the greater chance you'll have for the strongest teeth possible in the months and years to come.

Recap

- Maintaining oral health requires more frequent visits. Once every six months should now be once every three months.

- Dry mouth is a common occurrence. Drink water often and enthusiastically!
- Cancer treatments may lead to the need for restoration due to changes in the jaw bone.
- Special tools, like a fluoride tray that delivers prescription-level fluoride directly to your teeth, can help preserve and restore your oral health.
- Additionally, a customized shield can protect the parts of your mouth that don't need radiation.

Chapter Five:

Ongoing Care

Take control. Now is the time for you to chart a course of action if you're going to have treatments or if you've already finished treatments. You may experience symptoms like fatigue or nausea or just have a general uneasiness about the condition. Taking action can ease concerns during this time that may seem daunting. Start with the basics and make sure you master them.

Think of an all-star baseball player who plays second base. He's got great reflexes and has a quick throw to get an out. But the reason he's an all-star is because he does the basics well. If a ground ball is hit hard, he can drop to one knee, snag the hit, and toss to first base for the out.

Have you ever gone to a little kid's game? A ball is hit and as it rolls along, the player has the glove a couple feet off the ground and stares helplessly as the ball trickles between the legs and into the outfield. Young players have to master the basics.

Now it's your turn. In elementary school, the school nurse or health teacher may have shown a film or video on how to brush and floss. Kids' stuff, right? Yep, it is and for a good reason. As we've read, brushing and flossing well keeps harmful bacteria from lounging around the teeth and decaying the enamel. This basic instruction is something that all of us need to practice throughout our lives. It only costs several dollars a year, takes a few minutes a day and yet provides a foundation for our health, even with the complications that oral cancer can cause. Take a closer look.

Brush – What Type, How To Brush

Brush your teeth and tongue gently after each meal and at bedtime. Use a small, soft-bristle toothbrush and be sure you stop at the lining of the gums since you don't want to tear it. If your mouth is too sore for a regular soft toothbrush, you can get a super soft one from a drugstore. Some examples of these are:

- Biotene® Supersoft Toothbrush
- Sensodyne® Extra Soft, Gentle Toothbrush
- Colgate® 360 Sensitive Pro-Relief Toothbrush, Compact Head, Extra Soft
- Oral-B® Indicator 35 Compact Head Toothbrush, Soft

Don't grind your bristles into nothing. Change your toothbrush every three to four months or more often if needed.

Use a fluoride toothpaste or baking soda with fluoride. If you have a set of dentures, a bridge, or a dental prosthesis, take it out and clean it each time you clean your mouth. You can keep wearing it if it fits well and isn't irritating. Take it out of your mouth while you sleep. If you develop any irritation, keep it out of your mouth as much as possible.

Flossing

Floss your teeth with unwaxed dental floss once daily at bedtime. If you have not flossed regularly before treatment, don't start flossing now since it may cause bleeding. It's something we should talk about.

Some say flossing isn't beneficial, but it is a proven way to remove food particles lodged in tight places that toothbrushes often miss. Your teeth won't have the same exact spacing as someone else, like a family member or friend. If your teeth have some gaps then food particles may slip through and not get caught. The goal is keeping the teeth and gums clean to reduce the buildup of plaque and bacteria. If you have tight spaces, then flossing is a good idea.

Now here's a helpful tip from the Memorial Sloan Kettering Cancer Center in New York, where I spent a year as a fellow through the American Cancer Society. A little rinse goes a long way in keeping the mouth healthy.

Rinsing

Rinse your mouth every 4 to 6 hours, or more often as needed. Use one of the rinses listed below:

- One quart (4 cups) of water mixed with 1 teaspoon of salt and 1 teaspoon of baking soda
- One quart of water mixed with 1 teaspoon of salt
- One quart of water mixed with 1 teaspoon of baking soda
- Water

- A mouthwash with no alcohol or sugar, such as Biotene® PBF Oral Rinse or BetaCell™ Oral Rinse

Note: Don't use very hot or cold temperatures for mouth rinses.

Swish and gargle well for 15 to 30 seconds, then spit out the rinse.

If your nurse told you to irrigate your mouth, you will get other instructions about rinsing.

Please note: *If you have vomited from the effects of chemotherapy, don't brush your teeth right away. Instead, rinse with the baking soda rinse or even use plain water so that you reduce the acid in the mouth. This way, you're not scrubbing tooth-eroding acid into your teeth.*

Wet Your Lips

- Use a lip moisturizer (such as, Aquaphor®, Vaseline®, Eucerin Original®, or A&D® ointment).
- Do not apply lip moisturizers four hours before radiation therapy to the head and neck.

Toothpaste and Fluoride

We want you to be successful and what seems like little things does indeed matter, like the toothpaste you use. There are products created specifically for conditions like yours.

- Biotene® PBF Toothpaste
- Biotene® Antibacterial Dry Mouth Toothpaste
- Biotene® Gentle Mint Dry Mouth Toothpaste

- Squigle® Enamel Saver Toothpaste

What's the big deal about fluoride? Fluoride is a natural mineral that protects and "remineralizes" tooth enamel in areas that have been decalcified by acids. Plaque produces acids that cause the loss of minerals from the tooth, resulting in tooth decay. The formation of small cavities, or carious lesions, can be reversed by remineralization--that is, minerals that are deposited into previously damaged areas of tooth. Topical fluoride, when applied frequently in low concentrations, increases both the rate of growth and the size of enamel crystals.

Check-Ups

Stop in to the office every three months so I can see how well you're doing with your brushing and flossing in addition to doing an exam. Remember, my purpose is to find anything out of place so we can stop infections before they start.

What You Eat – Nutrition

Your food can improve your oral health by changing the pH of the mouth's environment. What you eat definitely matters. The right combination of proteins, fats, vegetables, carbohydrates, and water for staying hydrated will make your cancer treatment easier, and your recovery time shorter.

"Let your medicine be your food and your food be your medicine" is a quote attributed to Hippocrates. He was an important figure in the history of medicine because he was among the earliest to assert that diseases were caused by natural processes rather than the gods. He carefully documented patient histories and noted the physical findings.

It's often thought that good food is expensive and not affordable. However, stop in any grocery store and compare the prices of fresh fruits and vegetables with bags of potato chips and bags of candy. The fresh foods are much more affordable and you don't have to buy a lot at a time—and you don't have to shop at the upscale stores, either. Be practical, not fancy.

This is not an endorsement but stores like Super King, Sprouts, and Trader Joes carry high-quality produce at good prices. Even the 99 Cents Only stores will have fruits and veggies which can work if you're out and about and don't want to stop in a fast food restaurant. Of course, Whole Foods is among the most recognizable places to shop.

What If Chewing Is Uncomfortable?

Mouth irritations are common for oral cancer patients, so if chewing food is uncomfortable you can drink your meals. A counter-top appliance like a Vitamix® is versatile and does an excellent job of turning fruits and veggies into smoothies and hot soups.

Immersion blenders are also useful and convenient. They're a one-unit blender that you hold with one hand and use in a bowl that has ingredients for soups and sauces.

Want to turn your favorite fruits and veggies into a smoothie? Cut up peaches, oranges, and whatever else you want. Put them in a canister or tumbler that you're going to drink from and put the immersion blender to work. In seconds, your drink is ready and clean up with the one unit is convenient.

There is a reason behind eating well. Understanding this can boost your motivation to take in the foods that are good for you. Mucosal cells in our mouths turn over within three to seven days. So nutrient shortfalls or excesses will show up in mouth tissue before they show up anywhere else.

Periodontal disease is associated with lower blood levels of vitamins and minerals. And getting proper nutrients is important for successful treatment.

Lean meat like chicken, turkey, fish and low-fat dairy products are good sources of protein and are easy to eat.

And, yes, there are foods to avoid like salt, fat, alcohol, and sugar. These are empty calories.

Some Tips:

- Rinse your mouth with water before eating
- Avoid spicy foods and strong aromas
- Eat small, frequent meals so you don't feel deprived and your body can digest well
- Drink natural lemon-flavored drinks to stimulate saliva production
- Suck on ice chips and popsicles for a dry mouth condition

Disordered eating can get in the way of you pursuing the best oral health possible. Foods high in sugar and fat can increase the risk of enamel loss, lesions, dysfunctional salivation, swelling, and sensitivity.

Why the Right Food Is Important

What do you need for healthy teeth and gums, and why? Here's a handy chart:

NUTRIENT	BENEFITS
Protein	Helps develop strong teeth, mucosal cells and connective tissue that aid against bacteria and dehydration. A diet with the proper amount of protein aids in fights against infections.
Calcium	Strengthens the enamel that protects teeth from decay and erosion.
Phosphorus	Helps the body absorb calcium. Phosphate is a major component of our bone structure, it gives us energy, and synthesizes proteins, fats, and carbohydrates.
Zinc, Iron, Folate, Antioxidants	Zinc fights bacteria and plaque buildup, while iron and folate strengthen connective tissues. Antioxidants can help heal and repair the lining of the cheeks, tongue and gums.
Vitamin A	Aids in saliva production and keeps mucous membranes healthy.
Vitamin C	Strengthens the connective tissues that hold the teeth firmly in place.
Omega 3 animal-based fats like krill oil and fish oil	Important for reducing chronic inflammation.
Vitamin D	Plays an important role in enamel remineralization and helps the body to absorb calcium.
Vitamin B	Vitamin B3, Niacin; B2, Riboflavin; and B12 fight off

	inflammation in the mouth and battle against mouth sores. A feeling of a "burning mouth" may be due to a lack of Vitamin B.

Eat mostly a whole food diet with lots of lean protein and fresh vegetables.

Probiotics may help to decrease gingivitis and plaque; bacteria in fermented foods might suppress the growth of pathogens in the oral cavity. One study showed that consuming fermented dairy was associated with less periodontal diseases. Probiotics from any source could be helpful in a similar way.

Berry Bites

Cranberries and other plant foods rich in anthocyanins such as blueberries, raspberries, red cabbage, eggplant peel, and black rice may prevent pathogens from growing and flourishing on host tissues, including teeth.

Recap

- Back to basics: brush your teeth with a soft-bristle brush if your mouth is too sore for one with regular bristles. Do not forego brushing!
- In addition to brushing, flossing and rinsing must be part of your daily routine… and not necessarily limited to once a day.

- Yes, nutrition affects your oral health in addition to your overall well-being by changing the pH in your mouth's environment.
- If chewing is uncomfortable, start blending your meals into soups and smoothies.
- Make sure you include lean protein and fresh vegetables along with plenty of berries in your diet.

Chapter Six:

Staying Positive

Can you see how managing your oral health makes it possible for you to live as healthy as you possibly can? Keep this in mind. You don't have to suffer long-term oral complications from cancer treatment if you take charge and let me guide you in the right direction. Embrace a lifestyle of having the best oral health possible and you'll discover lasting benefits. Read on to see what I mean.

Your Calendar

I'm sure your days and weeks fill up, so guard this time to schedule an exam and cleaning once every few months. It's easy to let life crowd this out. You're recovering, but remember that your mouth's environment is in a fragile state and we want to restore it and keep it as vibrant as possible.

Feeling Great? Keep at It!

We often think that if we're feeling well then we don't need to see the dentist, doctor, chiropractor, or whoever cares for us. Don't react to your symptoms, stay a step ahead. If you're feeling great, then that's wonderful. Keep up your care because conditions can change without warning.

People who have been hiking in a place like the Rocky Mountains know this all too well. Experienced hikers and backpackers know how to be prepared. Novices can get fooled, especially if they're out on a trail that's bathed in sunshine. White puffy clouds float over the mountain ridges. They left their windbreaker or rain gear in the car because the weather looked so nice. And then, without warning, a storm cloud comes rolling in and they get soaked in a brief but heavy downpour.

A lifestyle of caring for your oral health means that you go through the paces of cleaning at home, using a fluoride tray, staying hydrated, and coming in for regular cleanings and exams. If you get a clean bill of health then great! If I see something that looks unusual or out of place, then we catch it early and can take action to prevent further infections from occurring.

Don't Feel Great? Let's Talk

> **"Strength does not come from physical capacity. It comes from an indomitable will."**
>
> **~ Mahatma Gandhi**

You've faced plenty of ups and downs to know that life is either like a roller coaster or a road with gently rolling hills. Change happens. Sometimes weekly, sometimes daily. If you don't feel well, for whatever reason, you can talk to me. We can look in your mouth for clues and if you need to unburden, I completely understand. I hope to earn enough of your trust and respect that you can feel comfortable in my office.

Stay Positive

Be diligent as you brush and floss. Use the self-care of your mouth to encourage and give you confidence. Develop a positive attitude, one where you know you're facing challenges and you're determined to remain at your best. How do you this? You can develop your own personal style. People of faith may decide to pray and become involved with serving others in their faith community. It's as easy as ever to listen to realistic yet positive messages. Download audio books from your local library or look up motivational speakers like Jim Rohn and Tony Robbins on YouTube. Several minutes of positive messages per day can fortify your attitude.

Control Your Stress Response

You've been through a major life event and now you're working on improving your condition. The stresses you experience simply don't go away so you can focus on your health. This is why an oral health lifestyle is necessary. It has a positive effect. Nothing is going to knock you off your game. Work on controlling your response. Look ahead in your week and see the most important tasks that you need to address. Ask for help as necessary and stay in communication with friends and family. Our bodies are a connected whole and so are our lives.

Find Support

We live in such a busy society that people come and go in our lives as they're zipping off to their own commitments. If you're in a crisis mode, then family and friends may slowly fade away or they'll want to give you all kinds of advice. Find someone who will take time to listen so you can freely share.

You may have to look outside of your current circle of friends and family. Listening does take skill and thought.

Check a site like Meetup.com for supportive groups and ones where they get together for light-hearted fun. They don't have to be recovering from a type of cancer. Maybe it's hiking or having an occasional dinner together. Having support may mean that you're looking for something positive to do with someone else.

> **"Never, never, never give up."**
>
> **~ Winston Churchill**

Specific Support

Your situation is unique and hearing from others who are dealing with recovery from either oral cancer or their own type can certainly be insightful. Here are some online resources, starting with my own website:

Dr. Ron Koslowski: comprehensive dental care with a cancer specialty.

www.KoslowskiDDS.com

Oral Cancer Foundation:

oralcancerfoundation.org/resources

Support for People with Oral and Head and Neck Cancer: www.spohnc.org

In Los Angeles, a comprehensive website is Los Angeles Cancer Advocacy and Support Groups:

www.lacancernetwork.com/advocacy-and-support-groups

Other regional ones with links to additional resources:

Memorial Sloan Kettering Cancer Center:

www.mskcc.org

Indiana University Oral Health Care for Cancer Patients:

www.dentistry.iu.edu/OHCCP/resources_cancer

Event: Cycle for Survival:

www.cycleforsurvival.org/

This indoor spinning cycle event takes place at Equinox gym locations across the nation. It's always inspirational and fun.

This event is the fastest growing fundraiser in the country, and along with the other locations across the nation we collectively raised over $164 million dollars for Memorial Sloan Kettering Cancer Center since the charity started in 2007. 100 percent of every dollar raised goes to pioneering research led by Memorial Sloan Kettering, the world's oldest and largest private cancer center.

This amazing charity was started by my cousin, Jennifer Goodman-Linn. Jen lost her long battle with cancer, but her incredible legacy lives on as does her memory which is a blessing to so many.

Check your local library for listings of meetings and a catalogue of other resources.

Be a Leader

Now reach out to others. After treatment, you'll be learning a lot as you go through your care plan. The tips and information you've picked up from reading this book are ones you can pass along to others in a similar situation. Since oral cancers often come from tobacco use and drinking alcohol, you can encourage others to not smoke and only drink in moderation. If they need help cutting back or quitting then offer to hold them accountable. Don't take on too much, though, so direct them to other supportive groups that you've found or show them how to look for help.

Teach others to look for the signs of oral cancer like swelling on one side of the neck. Don't wait. Have them see a physician immediately or to stop by my office for an exam.

Recap

- Put your scheduled visit on your calendar and guard that time. Don't let "life getting in the way" cause you to miss your checkup.
- If you feel great… great, but don't get lulled into slacking on your oral hygiene routines.
- Not feeling great? Let's talk.
- Stay positive with motivational readings, podcasts, etc.
- Find the support you need to help control stress – including outside your normal social circle of family and friends.

Chapter Seven:

Keep Smiling

The world needs your smile. It's a rare treasure. If I could show you, side-by-side, your mouth and teeth alongside a family member or best friend, you'd find subtle differences that make your mouth and face unique. Your bites are different as are the shades of your enamel. The shape of your jaw is just slightly different, too. Your uniqueness is important to me. The more I've studied the mouth, the more that I've come to respect the important part it plays in our overall well-being which is why crafting solutions continues to be my passion.

I was born and raised in Los Angeles and stayed local to attend dental school at UCLA where I graduated in 1991. The UCLA School of Dentistry was more than a place to get an education. It was a journey of discovery where I realized my love for solving complex problems.

I then had the privilege to work as a hospital dentistry resident at Rancho Los Amigos National Rehabilitation Center in Downey. I gained incredible experience treating patients with challenging physical and mental disabilities. They were grappling with the effects of spinal injuries, head traumas, and strokes.

It's easy to think of dentists as working alone since patients typically don't see other health professionals walking in and out of our offices. The time at Rancho, though, gave me valuable experience as a member of the medical team with physicians, surgeons, speech pathologists, occupational and physical therapists, and with the cleft palate team.

Becoming a prosthodontist was a natural extension for my learning so I continued at UCLA and the Wadsworth VA Medical Center for a two-year residency in Advanced Prosthodontics. I was focused, as noted in this description of the profession from the American College of Prosthodontists:

Prosthodontists are the recognized experts when anything needs to be replaced in your mouth. This can range from a single tooth, multiple teeth, or all teeth and gums in the mouth. While many other dentists can do some of these treatments, prosthodontists are the specialists dedicated to this type of care.

But that wasn't enough to satisfy my curiosity. Dentistry is a helping profession and I saw how working with oral cancer patients could bring hope and change lives.

Soon after that, my next stop was the Memorial Sloan Kettering Cancer Center in New York City, consistently named as the world's finest cancer treatment center with an environment that's supportive for the patients and for the professionals working there. It's an optional year for prosthodontists who want the additional training in caring for cancer patients.

I consider it an honor to have spent a year of my life as a fellow, sponsored by the American Cancer Society and working exclusively with cancer patients. I'm drawn to the functional, aesthetic, and medical aspects of my work, so it was great to be part of the medical team. The sole focus that year was taking care of the dental needs of cancer patients, but it also equipped me to work with a variety of medical professionals.

The intensive training and knowledge enhanced my skills in Maxillofacial Prosthetics, looking at the mouth in new ways and witnessing the benefit of restorations for the teeth, gums, and other oral structures. I worked on advanced cases and saw up close how my profession gives patients hope, too. I became board certified in the specialty of prosthodontics in 2000, but that wasn't the culmination of my learning. That continues along with my pursuit of excellence for each patient.

> **"Optimism is the faith that leads to achievement. Nothing can be done without hope and confidence."**
>
> **~ Helen Keller**

This is a wonderful era to work in with advances made in techniques like radiation treatment, ongoing studies in DNA, prevention and treatment. The American Cancer Society reports that one of the changes often found in DNA of oral cancer cells is a mutation of a specific gene. Changes in the *TP53* gene can lead to increased growth of abnormal cells and cancer. Research is being done on gene therapy to boost the immune system so it can better find and kill cancer cells. These forms of treatment are still in very early stages of study.

While research continues, let's talk about what concerns you. Prevention. Being a partner with you in pursuing better health is my greatest reward, and I'd like to leave you with this important truth: Identifying and addressing problems before they reach an advanced stage is key. That's how you can best leverage my specialty in caring for patients with the complex needs brought about by oral cancer.

The same attitude is found in the restorative dentistry services I provide, as well.

Not everyone who comes to me has a complicated dental problem, but they've discovered how my patients trust me.

The discipline of prosthodontics is one of nine specialties recognized by the American Dental Association. To earn my degree, I invested an extensive number of hours in classroom lectures and seminars, plus many hours of lab and clinical training. Topics covered include aesthetics and cosmetics, bridges, veneers, inlays, complete and removable partial dentures, dental implants and studying how teeth were affected by genetics or at birth.

As a prosthodontist, I also care for patients with snoring and disorders like sleep apnea. I can provide specific devices as alternatives to a CPAP mask that is comfortable and without being annoying and improve on what someone may be using.

Quality and artistry are hallmarks of my work and so is doing procedures right the first time. The old adage of "measure twice, cut once" really does apply. I see it firsthand since I'm asked to re-do work that other dental professionals attempted but did not perform to the patient's satisfaction.

Early in my career, I promised to do the absolute best for my patients and so there are some things I don't do in my practice. For one, I like to share what dental insurance is all about. It's really more of a contract between one's employer and the insurance company. Dentists who provide treatment on this model see patients in volume and that takes away from the individualized attention that they can give.

I also refuse to run ads that make it sound like I'm having a sale on procedures like implants. These are often bait and switch to get you in the door and then you're told that you're not a candidate for the deal that was offered.

Patient's needs are customized so consultation and careful planning lay the ground work for setting expectations and understanding the necessary procedures to improve your oral health. This is how I offer my skilled craftsmanship so that your mouth is restored, giving you the confidence to go out in public and talk up close and personal with loved ones. You have something to offer those around you—yourself, and the gift of your smile. And your inspiration to step out and become confident in who you are motivates me to continue caring for others.

> **"With the new day comes new strength and new thoughts."**
>
> **~ Eleanor Roosevelt**

Resources

Use the important information in this section to compile all of your own personal information. Plus you will find a handy quick-reference guide reprinted with permission from the National Institute of Health. And at the very end, you'll find pages on which you can jot your own notes.

My Cancer Care Team

Share the following information and numbers with everyone on your team:

My number: ________________________________

My Partner/Caregiver:

Name:____

Number: ____

My Cancer Doctor/Oncologist:

Name: ____

Number: ____

My Radiologist:

Name:______________________________________

Number: ____________________________________

My Nurse:

Name: ______________________________________

Number: ____________________________________

My Dentist/Dental Hygienist:

Name: ______________________________________

Number: ____________________________________

My Social Worker:

Name: ______________________________________

Number: ____________________________________

Other Important Numbers (Toll-free):

National Oral Health Information Clearing House:
1-877-216-1019

Cancer Information Service:
1-800-422-6237

Remember:

For your pre-treatment dental exam, ask your cancer doctor or radiologist to send the following information to your dentist/prosthodontist:

- Your diagnosis
- Your blood counts
- Important head and neck X-rays
- Your treatment plans:
  - Radiation therapy
  - Chemotherapy

Oral Health, Cancer Care, and You

Fitting the Pieces Together

Three Good Reasons to See a Dentist BEFORE Cancer Treatment:

1. **Feel Better:** Cancer treatment can cause side effects in your mouth. A dental checkup before treatment starts can help prevent painful mouth problems.
2. **Save teeth and bones:** A dentist will help protect your mouth, teeth, and jaw bones from damage caused by head and neck radiation and chemotherapy. Children also need special protection for their growing teeth and facial bones.
3. **Fight cancer:** Serious side effects in the mouth can delay, or even stop, cancer treatment. To fight cancer best, your cancer care team should include a dentist.

Protect your mouth during cancer treatment

Brush gently, brush often

- Brush your teeth—and your tongue—gently with an extra soft toothbrush.
- Soften the bristles in warm water if your mouth is very sore.
- Brush after every meal and at bedtime.

Floss gently—do it daily

- Floss once a day to remove plaque.
- Avoid areas of your gums that are bleeding or sore, but keep flossing your other teeth.

Keep your mouth moist

- Rinse often with water.
- Don't use mouthwashes that contain alcohol.
- Use a saliva substitute to help moisten your mouth.

Eat and drink with care

- Choose soft, easy-to-chew foods.
- Protect your mouth from spicy, sour, or crunchy foods.
- Choose lukewarm foods and drinks instead of hot or icy-cold ones.
- Avoid alcoholic drinks.

Stop using tobacco

- Ask your cancer care team to help you stop smoking or chewing tobacco. People who quit smoking or chewing tobacco have fewer mouth problems.

Tips to help you care for mouth problems

Sore Mouth, Sore Throat

To help keep your mouth clean, rinse often with ¼ teaspoon of salt and ¼ teaspoon of baking soda in 1 quart (4 cups) of warm water. Follow with a plain water rinse. Ask your cancer care team about medicines that can help with the pain.

Dry Mouth

Rinse your mouth often with water, use sugar-free gum or candy, and talk to your dentist about saliva substitutes.

Infections

Call your cancer care team right away if you see a sore, swelling, bleeding, or a sticky, white film in your mouth.

Eating Problems

Your cancer care team can help by giving you medicines to numb the pain from mouth sores and showing you how to choose foods that are easy to swallow.

Bleeding

If your gums bleed or hurt, avoid flossing the areas that are bleeding or sore, but keep flossing the other teeth. Soften the bristles of your toothbrush in warm water.

Stiffness in Chewing Muscles

Three times a day, open and close your mouth as far as you can without pain. Repeat 20 times.

Vomiting

Rinse your mouth after vomiting with ¼ teaspoon of baking soda in 1 cup of warm water.

Cavities

Brush your teeth after meals and before bedtime. Your dentist might have you put fluoride gel on your teeth to help prevent cavities.

When should you call your cancer care team about mouth problems?

Take a moment each day to check how your mouth looks and feels.

Call your cancer care team when:

- ✓ You first notice a mouth problem.
- ✓ An old problem gets worse.
- ✓ You notice any changes you're not sure about.

For additional copies contact:

National Institute of Dental and Craniofacial Research

National Oral Health Information Clearinghouse

1 NOHIC Way

Bethesda, MD 20892-3500

1-866-232-4528

www.nidcr.nih.gov

NIH Publication No. 15-5494

Sept. 2015

NIH... Turning Discovery Into Health®

About the Author

Ronald Koslowski, D.D.S., F.A.C.P. was born and raised in Los Angeles. After graduating from UCLA School of Dentistry in 1991, Dr. Koslowski completed specialty training in Advanced Prosthodontics at UCLA and the Wadsworth VA Medical Center.

From 1994 to 1995, Dr. Koslowski was an American Cancer Society Fellow in Maxillofacial Prosthetics at Memorial Sloan Kettering Cancer Center in New York City.

In 2000, Dr. Koslowski became board certified in the specialty of Prosthodontics and was named a Fellow of the American College of Prosthodontists (F.A.C.P.).

As a Lecturer at UCLA School of Dentistry, Dr. Koslowski has participated in the clinical training of dental students and specialty residents for over 15 years.

Dr. Koslowski maintains a private practice specializing in Prosthodontics, Maxillofacial Prosthetics, and Dental Oncology in Encino, California.

To contact Dr. Koslowski and schedule a consultation, visit his website (www.KoslowskiDDS.com) or call 818-986-9036.

About the Author

Notes:

Notes

Notes

Notes

Made in the USA
Monee, IL
26 June 2024

60472382R00059